Broad-tailed

Hummingbirds

Lois Lake

I want to thank Charlie and Rita Summers for being my photography mentors. They have taught me so much about how to create a good image, not just take a snapshot. They invited my husband and me on trips that we would not have otherwise taken and while on those trips I learned so much about photography just by being around them. Charlie and Rita are willing to share their expertise and coach me in a way that causes me to go beyond my comfort zone. I remember submitting an image for competition and critique to the Mile High Wildlife Photo Club and Charlie was the judge that night. He said, "I don't know who made this image but if they would like some tips on how to make it better, call me." I called and there were many times I thought he was talking a foreign language. At first, I did not understand the terminology, but both Charlie and Rita were very patient and answered my questions; both about taking the image and processing it.

I also want to thank Don Hopkins for telling us about the hummingbird nest and letting me hang out in his yard for hours at a time on many mornings and evenings, so I could watch the baby hummingbirds as they grew to become independent. This was an opportunity that very few people have, and I enjoyed so much sharing observations with Don as I photographed the nest in his yard.

The behavior that I observed stirred my curiosity and caused me to search the internet for more information about hummingbirds. I have added those little bits of knowledge to the pictures in this book to illustrate what I saw.

The most common hummingbird in Colorado is the Broad-tailed Hummingbird (Selasphorus platycercus). They typically spend the winter in Central America or Mexico and migrate north during the early spring. Around Mother's Day I saw the hummingbird hovering outside our kitchen window where we had the feeder the previous year. It was like he was saying, "I'm back. Where is the food?" The male arrives as much as three weeks before the female arrives. Quite often we will get a snowstorm after the hummingbird arrives.

Hummingbirds flap their wings about 80 times per second. It is so fast that they make a humming noise and that is how they got their name. The hummingbird's heartbeats can vary from about 250 beats per minute when it is resting to about 1200 beats per minute when it is feeding. Their body temperature is between 104 and 108 degrees. This fast heartbeat and body temperature require that they eat a lot and eat often.

Natural food is scarce in the early spring when the hummingbird arrives in Colorado. Indian Paintbrush (Castilleja) is one of the first flowers to bloom in May and its bright red color attracts the hummingbird.

Hummingbirds have a long and tapered bill that is used to obtain nectar from the center of long, tubular flowers. They have a long tongue which they use to lick their food at a rate of up to 13 licks per second.

Hummingbirds can fly right, left, up, down, backwards, and even upside down. They are also able to hover by flapping their wings in a figure-eight pattern.

Most people think hummingbirds only eat nectar, but they also get their nutrition from tree sap, spiders, bugs and pollen. I saw this hummingbird acting strange, so I started taking pictures to see if I could figure out what was happening. After I processed it on the computer I realized it was catching and eating a mosquito.

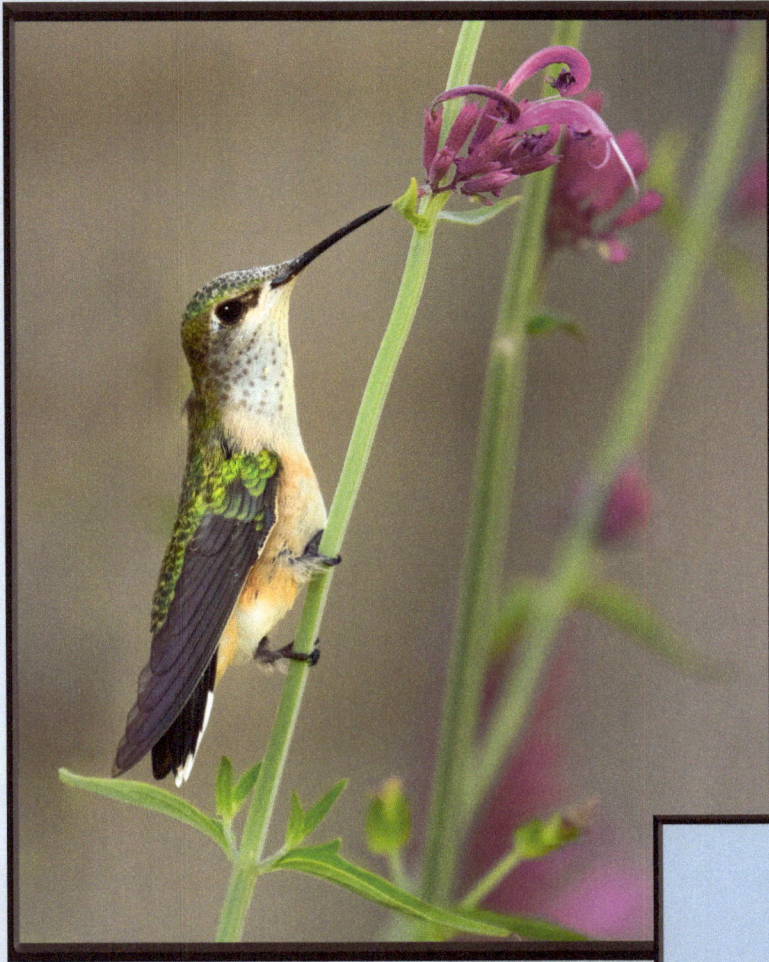

The hummingbird's feet are used for perching only and are not used for hopping or walking. One afternoon I saw her perched on the stem of the hummingbird mint looking for bugs.

Another time I saw her getting tree sap from the bristlecone pine tree.

When the female arrives, she starts looking for a place to build the nest. The female builds the nest by herself and it takes about a week. It is made of lichen, dead leaves and moss. She uses her saliva to glue the nesting material together. Then she gathers spider webbing to wrap around the nest and secure it to the branches. The spiderwebs give the nest elasticity so it can stretch as the babies grow.

Hummingbirds usually lay two eggs per clutch. They are about 1/2-inch-long and 1/3-inch-wide; about the size of a jelly bean. Generally, incubation is between fourteen and seventeen days.

When the babies hatch, their eyes are closed, they have no feathers. They are about an inch long and cannot regulate their body heat, so Mom stays with them for the first eight to twelve days. Only the mother participates in the nesting duties. If the male comes around the nest the female is afraid his bright-colored feathers will attract predators, so she chases him away.

The baby hummingbird is instinctively potty trained. It wiggles around until its little tail is above the side of the nest before it goes to the bathroom.

About nine days after they hatch, the baby's eyes open and their feathers are starting to develop. They have enough feathers to regulate their body temperature and the mother hummingbird will no longer need to sit on the nest all the time. She feeds them about every twenty to thirty minutes.

When the baby hummingbirds are two weeks old they are completely covered in pin feathers and are starting to grow real feathers. They have doubled in size. Their beaks are much longer and are starting to look much darker. They are beginning to look like real birds.

One morning I noticed when Mama fed the chicks, she didn't leave immediately. After feeding both chicks, she sat on top of them. I wondered if she was pushing them down to make them wiggle and exercise their wings to get stronger or if she was trying to stretch the nest to make more room for them. It looked like the nest was larger at the top than it was the last time I was here. The babies were getting so big it was a tight fit for both in the nest.

As the babies grew, they became more aware of their surroundings. They could tell when Mama was coming to the nest to feed them. Both immediately had their beaks open as if to say, "Me first, me first."

This morning the feeding seemed different. Mama inserted her beak in its mouth and then she bobbed her head up and down VERY quickly and went deeper than I noticed before. I read that most of their diet is partially-digested insects, regurgitated by the Mama and shoved directly down their throats all the way into their stomachs. She fed one and then the other. As soon as she finished feeding them, she left to find more food.

Preening is the bird's way of
keeping their feathers in
optimum condition. They preen
to remove any dust, parasites
or food particles that may
have gotten on their feathers.
Birds use their beak and feet
to preen their feathers and
get them in just the right
position, so they are
waterproofed and insulated
to protect against extreme
hot or cold temperatures.
Instinctively the babies knew
that they should preen their
feathers.

The baby used its long tongue
to clean its beak after being fed.

In a few weeks, the chicks are much larger and more alert. They are staying awake longer between feedings and stretching their wings more.

I photographed the baby hummingbirds every few days. One morning, one of the chicks was flapping its wings at full hummingbird speed. It looked like they were elbowing each other and saying, "stop pushing" or "you are crowding me." If they wanted to move around in the nest they almost had to do it in unison.

One morning when I arrived at the nest it was fifty-five degrees. It was cloudy and overcast. They had their feathers all fluffed up to keep warm.

The chicks no longer fit in the nest. Their heads stuck out one side and their tails hung over the other. If one moved, it ended up on top of the other chick. They could not flap their wings at the same time, so they took turns.

The Mama came in every ten to fifteen minutes to feed the chicks and they were much more active than other days. It made me think they needed more food to keep their body temperature up because of the cold weather. They were stretching and flapping their wings much more often.

The chicks were almost the size of the adult now and their feathers were almost fully developed.

Mama landed on one of the branches that allowed her to get more distance from the nest. The chicks were getting so big she had to feed them in a horizontal position instead of feeding them from above. She continued using a riveting motion when feeding the chicks. It reminded me of a woodpecker's motion when they are getting bugs from the tree.

At three weeks of age, the babies look more like real hummingbirds. They begin to stretch and exercise their wings in preparation for flight. They hang on to the floor of the nest, so they do not have to worry about accidentally flying away too soon. In the next few days, these little baby hummingbirds will fly away and never return to the nest.

Every time I visited I noticed they were stretching and flapping their wings more. They needed to practice flight and build strength in their wings.

I had been photographing the babies for about twenty-eight days when one morning I arrived at the nest and there was only one baby in the nest. The other chick had fledged. I watched the one still in the nest and it was stretching, looking over the edge of the nest and flapping its wings at full speed. I could tell it would not be long before it left the nest also. The chick looked at the branch to the left as if to say, "I wonder where that branch goes?"

After Mama came in to feed the chick it looked at the branches above it. Then it looked at the branches high and to the right. Pretty soon it turned around in the nest and looked at the branches above it and to the left. The expression on its face said, "I wonder if I could reach that branch? Or maybe that other one would be easier to get to." It looked over the edge of the nest and you could tell it was thinking, "That is a long way down."

I could hear Mama as she approached the nest to feed the chick. She landed on a branch about four feet up and to the left of the nest. I started looking around and found the chick that had fledged. The Mama was feeding that chick first and then she fed the chick in the nest.

The little chick on the branch waited and waited for Mama to bring food.

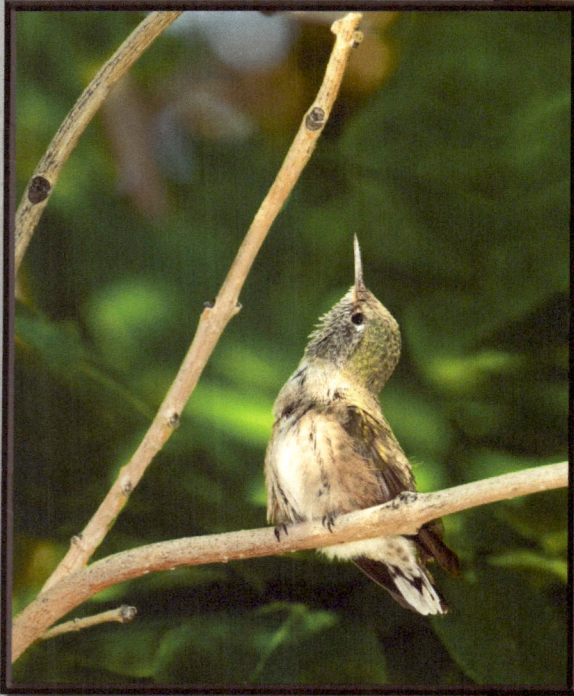

Every time it heard a sound it would look around to see if it was Mama with food.

Pretty soon it was so tired of waiting it was sound asleep on the branch.

The next time Mama came in to feed, she fed the chick up on the branch and then she landed on the branch by the nest, but she did not feed the chick in the nest. It was like she was saying, "I have food but if you want it, you have to come get it." She was trying to coax the other chick out of the nest.

The little chick
stretched and
flapped its wings.

It carefully inspected
its feathers as if it
wondered if they
would carry it to the
next branch.

After about
thirty minutes,
Mama came
back and fed
the little
chick still in
the nest.

When she left,
the baby settled
down for a nap. It
is a lot of work
to exercise your
wings and wonder
if your feathers
are developed
enough for flight.

The fledgling watched as its sibling prepared for flight. It was not very happy about the whole situation. If the sibling fledged also, then there would be less food for him. He made a big show of strength to defend his food source.

Throughout the day the
fledgling stretched and
flapped its wings.

It was just about
ready to take off
and then it would
change its mind
and grab on to
the branch again.

After exercising its wings, it would preen just as an adult bird would do to groom their feathers. Pretty soon it started flapping its wings and took off. It landed on another dead branch about two feet away. I looked around and Mama had chosen a perfect spot to raise her young.

There were plenty of branches within short distances for the chicks to get their wings ready for long flights and there were plenty of other trees nearby so with each flight they could extend their range.

Mama continues to feed the fledgling for two to three days after it leaves the nest. During this time, she will show it all the good places to catch bugs and get nectar. When they get good at finding their own food, she will chase them off to live on their own.

A few weeks after fledging, the juvenile male hummingbird starts to get the red color on his gorget. The gorget is the feathers at their throat that turn an iridescent color when the light hits them just right.

Agastache (pronounced a **gas** ta key) cana or 'Ava' Hummingbird Mint is very attractive to the hummingbird as well as people. If you brush up against it, you can smell the fragrant mint. The brilliant pink color draws the hummingbirds to it.

Hummingbirds have a long bill which allows them to get nectar from plants that other birds and insects cannot.

The brick on our house was in the shadow with the Hummingbird Mint in the sunlight. It made a beautiful backdrop to photograph the hummingbird when it came to feed.

The hummingbird reaches deep to get all the nectar. The Licorice Mint or sometimes called Sunset Hyssop (Agastache rupestris) is one of their favorite plants. It has a wonderful licorice fragrance and is very water-wise for our Colorado climate.

If I stood in just the right spot late in the afternoon I could get the sun shining on the dead pine needles for a backdrop that matched the color of the Sunset Hyssop. The tricky part was willing the hummingbird to come to the plant to feed during my thirty-minute window of opportunity.

Orange Carpet (Zauschneria) trumpet vine is just what it says. It grows low to the ground like a carpet. It is a water-wise plant that spreads readily. It is difficult to photograph the hummingbird on this plant, but occasionally you will get a bloom on a stem long enough to get a clean background.

Indian Paintbrush (Castilleja) is a parasite plant. Its roots attach to another living plant such as a grass and the paintbrush gets its water and nutrition from the host plant. They are very difficult to transplant and will not live without the host plant.

The Butterfly Bush (Buddleia) not only attracts butterflies but also attracts the hummingbirds. When it gets tired of flying it just sits down and has a sip of nectar from the blossom on the butterfly bush.

The days start getting shorter and colder in mid-September. The hummingbird's biological clock tells them it is time to fly south. The young hummingbirds are completely independent when it is time to migrate and they migrate without parental guidance. A hummingbird's heartbeat during migration is about twelve hundred beats per minute and their wings flap fifteen to eighty times per second. This high activity requires a lot of energy. They will gain twenty-five to forty percent of their body weight before they start migration. While migrating, they fly low to the ground, so they can readily see food sources and stop along the way.

I always love watching the hummingbirds but being able to photograph them in the nest made this year very special. I learned so much more about hummingbirds by observing their behavior and spending time with them. I look forward to them returning next year.

Photography is more than taking a picture for Lois. It is a connection with nature; a way to worship God and appreciate the beauty that God has created for us to enjoy. Photography causes her to look deeper, be more curious, learn more about her subject and try to bring the viewer on that journey with her.

Sometimes things happen in nature that leave us wondering, "Did I really see what I think I saw?" The high speed of the shutter captures many wonderful and fascinating moments that lead to further research and knowledge.

Lois likes to capture the stormy moods of nature and scenes of what happens in the outdoors. She is fascinated with communication and body language among wildlife and enjoys the challenge of trying to memorialize that connection in a photograph. Lois spends a lot of time studying her subjects to learn their behavior and anticipate their moves so she can capture the precise second of the desired action.

www.ingramcontent.com/pod-product-compliance
Lightning Source LLC
Chambersburg PA
CBHW041240020426
42333CB00002B/30

9 781943 650873